ASY PIANO

RODGERS & HAMMERSTEIN'S

THE KING AND I

ISBN 978-1-4950-2566-2

The offering of this publication for sale is not to be construed as authorization for the performance of any material contained herein.
Applications for the right to perform THE KING AND I, in whole or in part, should be addressed to:

R & H THEATRICALS
229 West 28th Street, 11th Floor
New York, New York 10001
Tel 800/400.8160 or 212/564.4000 * Fax 212/268.1245 * E-mail theatre @ rnh.com
www.rnh.com

Rodgers and Hammerstein is a trademark used under license from Rodgers and Hammerstein as licensee of Imagem, C.V.
Williamson Music is a registered trademark used under license from Rodgers and Hammerstein as licensee of Imagem, C.V.
The R&H logo is a trademark used under license from Rodgers and Hammerstein as licensee of Imagem, C.V.

WILLIAMSON MUSIC®

AN IMAGEM COMPANY™
www.rnh.com

HAL•LEONARD® CORPORATION

7777 W. BLUEMOUND RD. P.O. BOX 13819 MILWAUKEE, WI 53213

Visit Hal Leonard Online at
www.halleonard.com

GETTING TO KNOW YOU

Lyrics by OSCAR HAMMERSTEIN II
Music by RICHARD RODGERS

Moderately *(gracefully and not fast)*

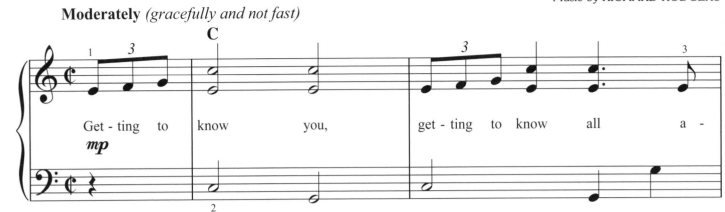

Get - ting to know you, get - ting to know all a -

bout you, get - ting to like you,

get-ting to hope you like me. Get-ting to

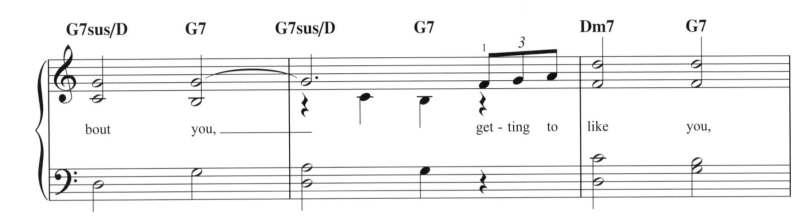

know you, put-ting it my way, but nice - ly,

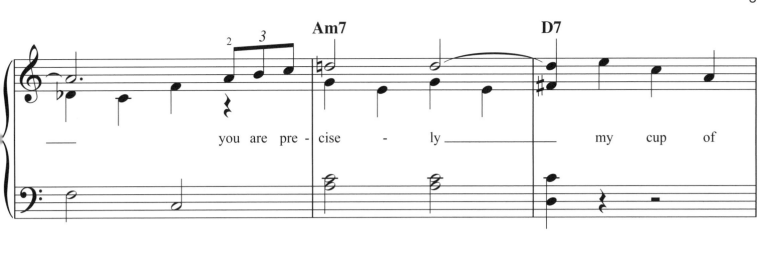

you are pre - cise - ly _____ my cup of

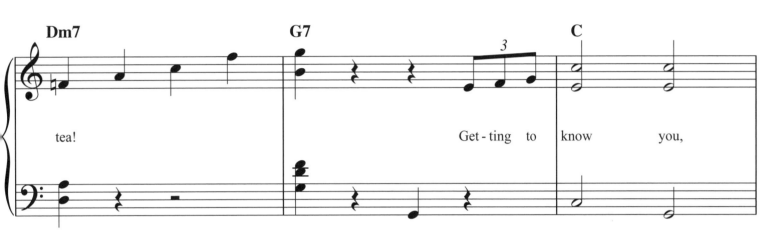

tea! Get - ting to know you,

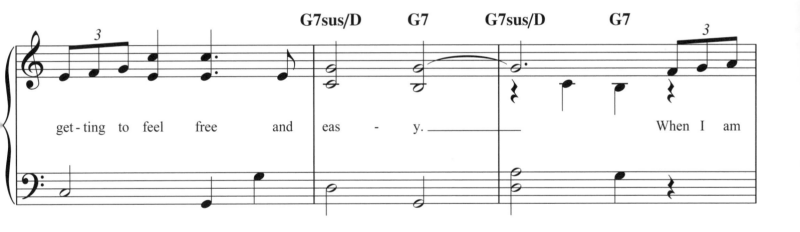

get - ting to feel free and eas - y. _____ When I am

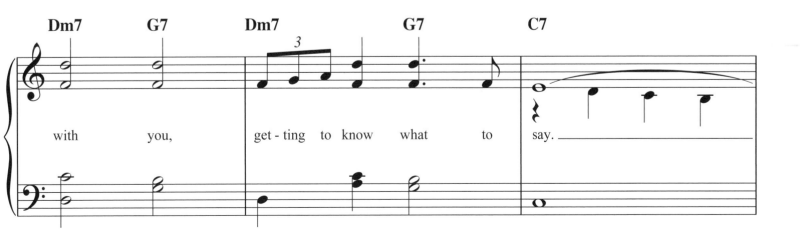

with you, get - ting to know what to say. _____

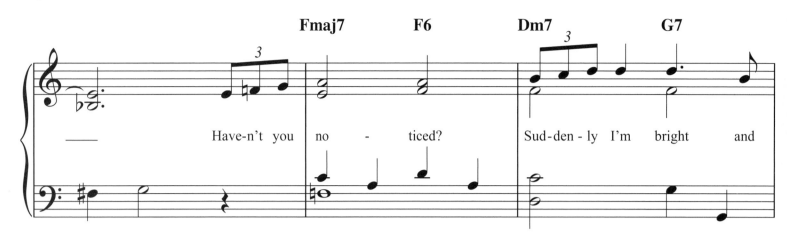

Fmaj7 F6 Dm7 G7

Have-n't you no - ticed? Sud-den-ly I'm bright and

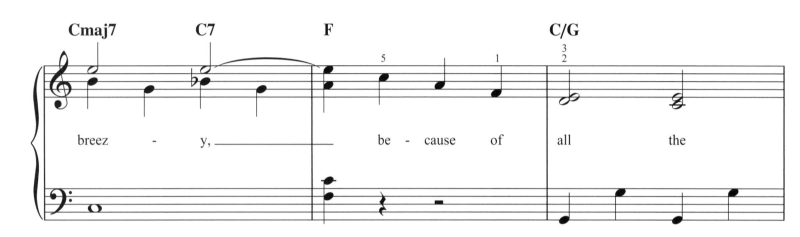

Cmaj7 C7 F C/G

breez - y, _____ be - cause of all the

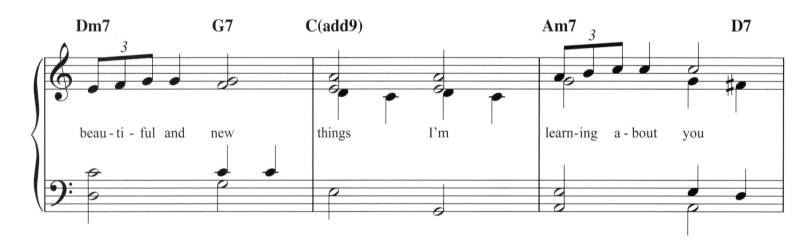

Dm7 G7 C(add9) Am7 D7

beau-ti - ful and new things I'm learn-ing a-bout you

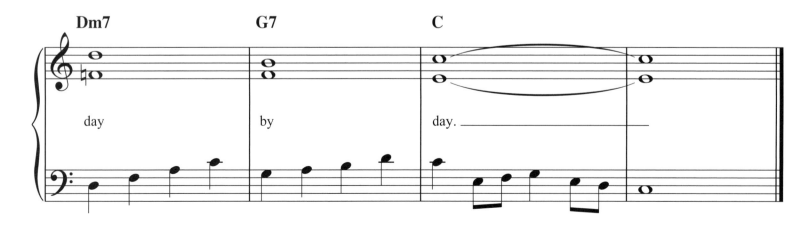

Dm7 G7 C

day by day. _____

HELLO, YOUNG LOVERS

Lyrics by OSCAR HAMMERSTEIN II
Music by RICHARD RODGERS

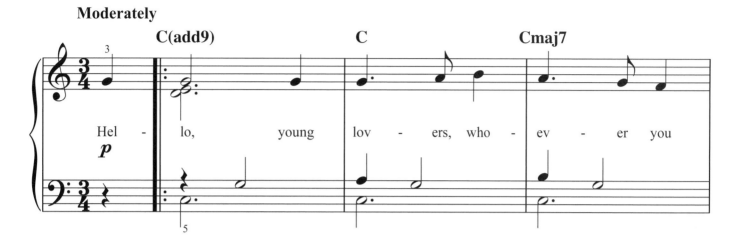

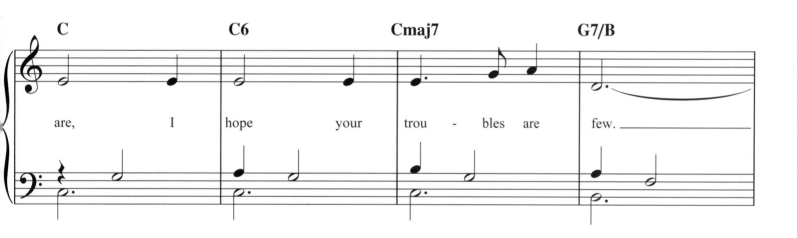

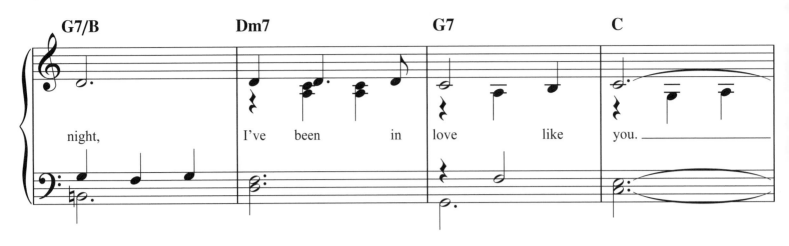

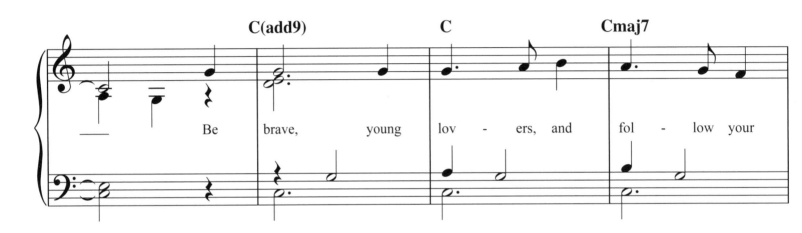

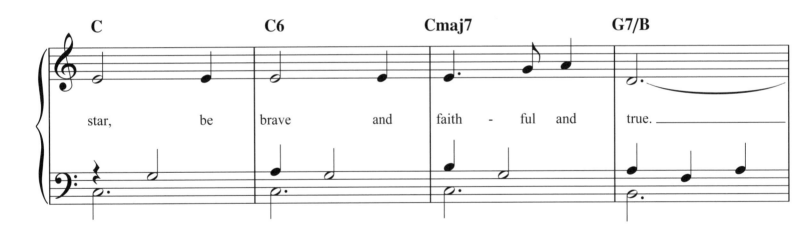

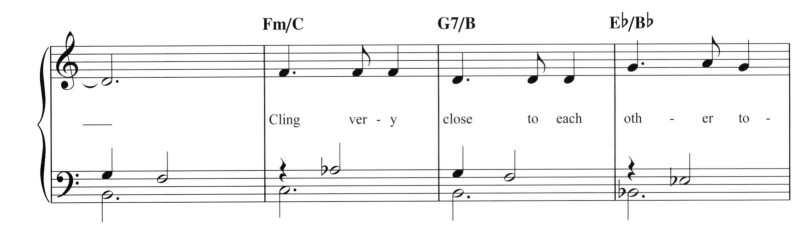

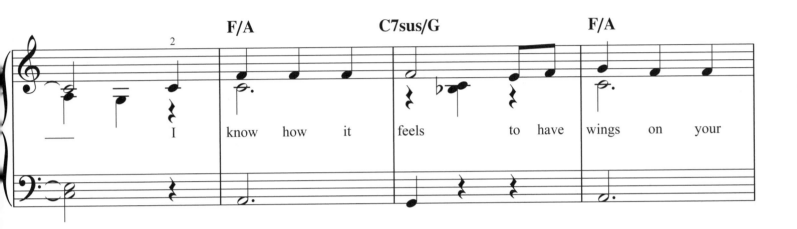

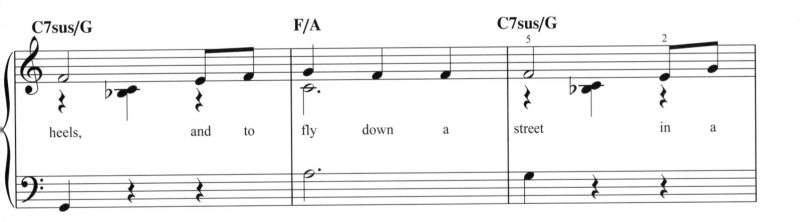

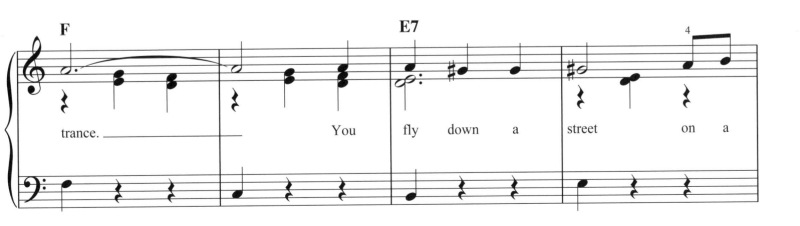

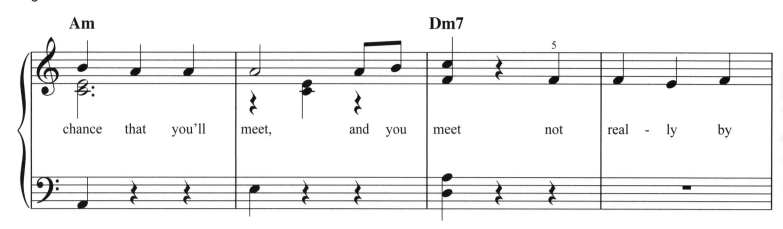

chance that you'll meet, and you meet not real - ly by

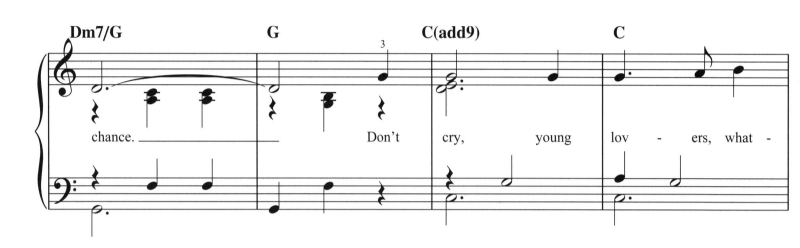

chance. Don't cry, young lov - ers, what -

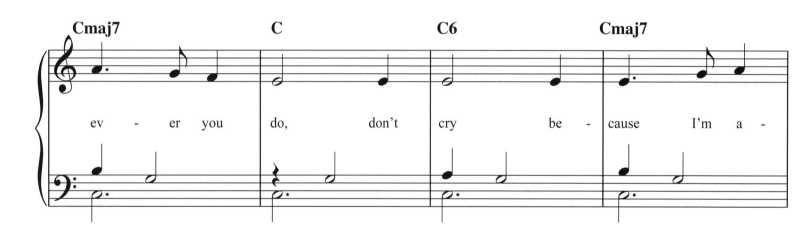

ev - er you do, don't cry be - cause I'm a -

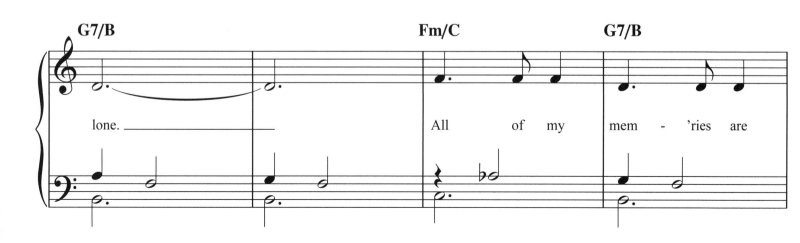

lone. All of my mem - 'ries are

E♭/B♭   **G7/B**   **Dm7**   **G**

hap - py to - night,   I've had a   love of my

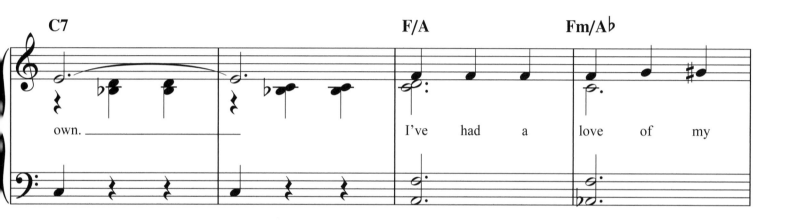

C7   **F/A**   **Fm/A♭**

own.   I've had a   love of my

C/G   **Dm7**   **E♭/G**   **G7**

own,   like yours.   I've had a   love of my

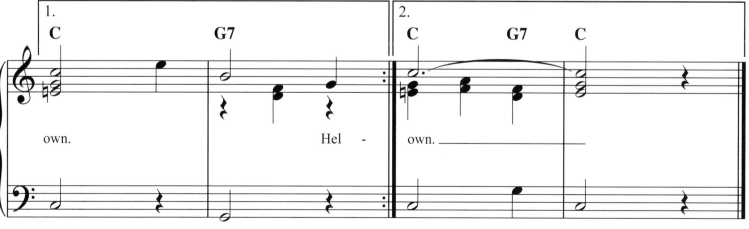

1.   **C**   **G7**   2.   **C**   **G7**   **C**

own.   Hel -   own.

I HAVE DREAMED

Lyrics by OSCAR HAMMERSTEIN II
Music by RICHARD RODGERS

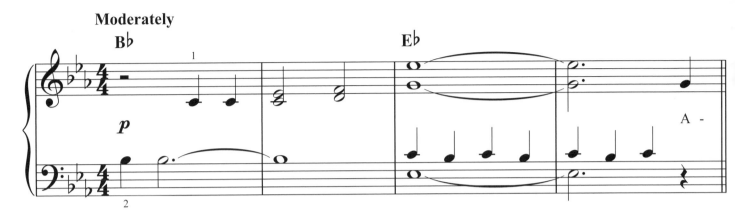

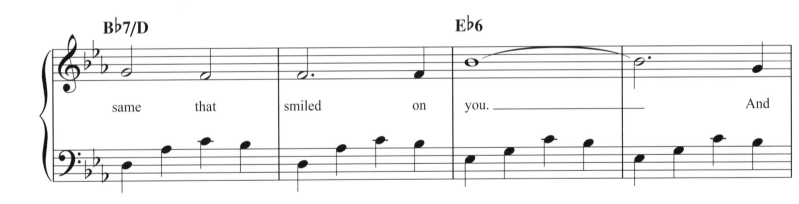

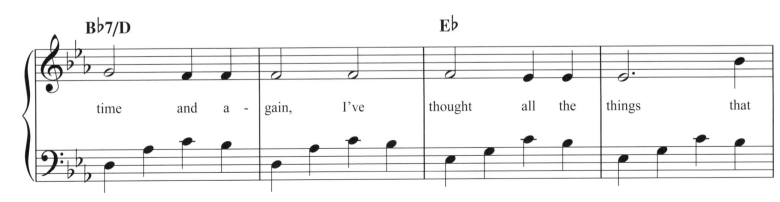

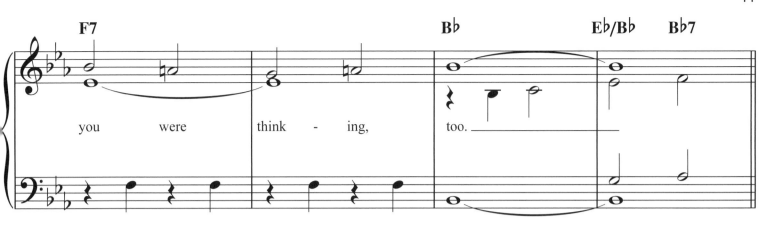

you were think - ing, too.

Slowly, very smoothly

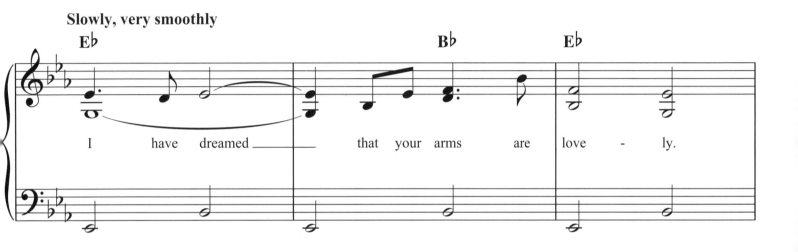

I have dreamed that your arms are love - ly.

I have dreamed what a joy you'll

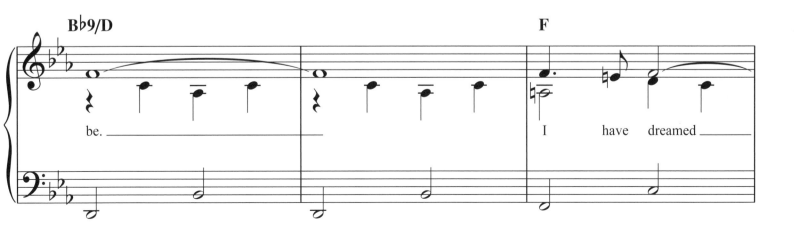

be. I have dreamed

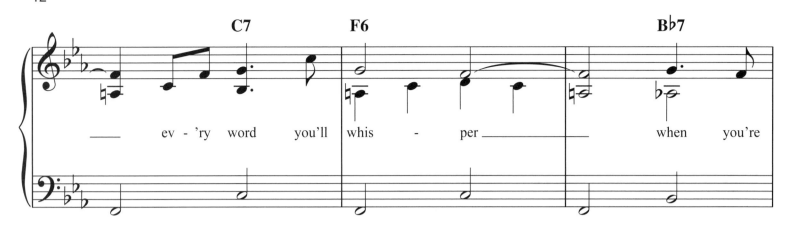

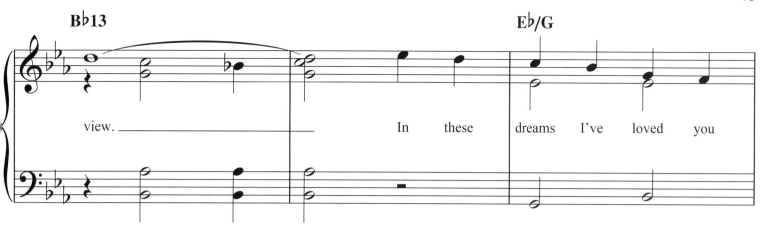

view. _____ In these dreams I've loved you

so, that by now I think I know what it's

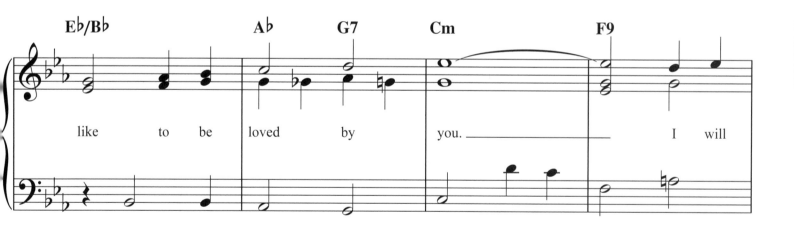

like to be loved by you. _____ I will

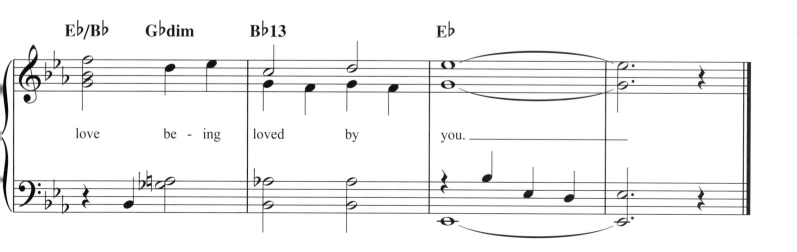

love be - ing loved by you. _____

I WHISTLE A HAPPY TUNE

Lyrics by OSCAR HAMMERSTEIN II
Music by RICHARD RODGERS

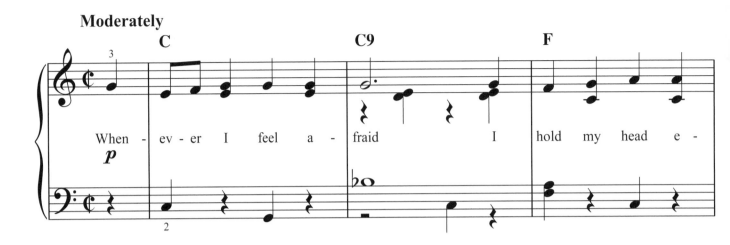

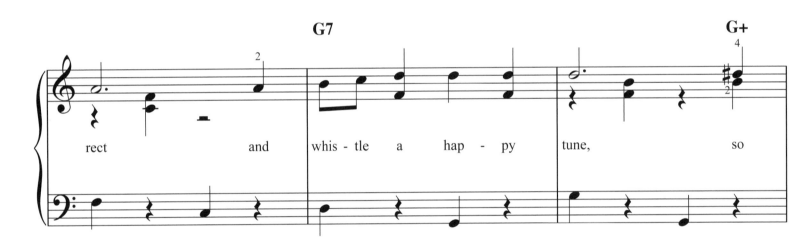

While shiv - er - ing in my shoes, I

strike a care - less pose and whis - tle a hap - py

tune and no one ev - er knows I'm a -

fraid. The re - sult of this de -

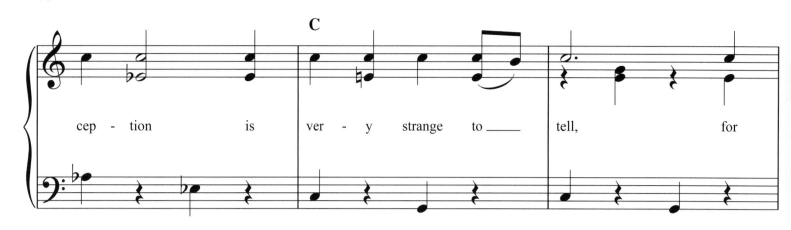

cep - tion   is   ver - y strange to ____ tell,   for

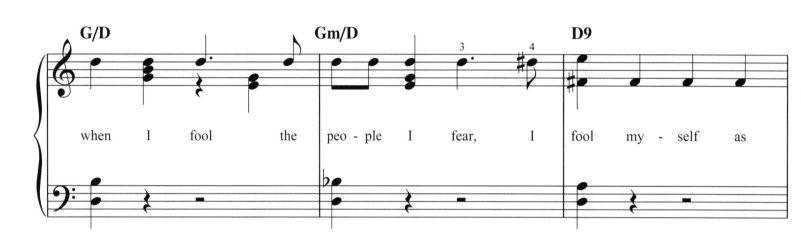

when I fool   the   peo - ple I fear, I   fool my - self as

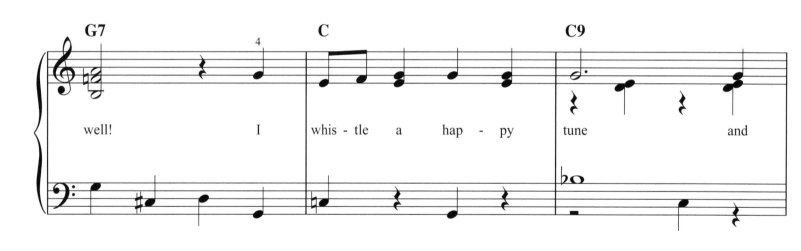

well!   I   whis - tle a hap - py   tune   and

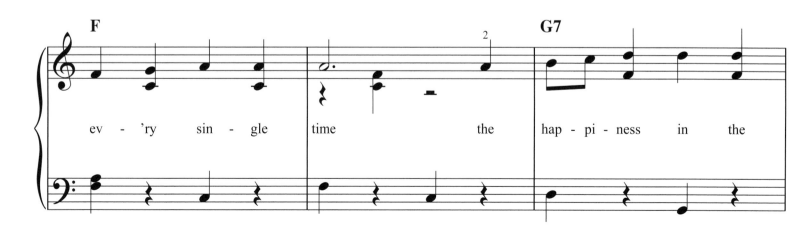

ev - 'ry sin - gle   time   the   hap - pi - ness in the

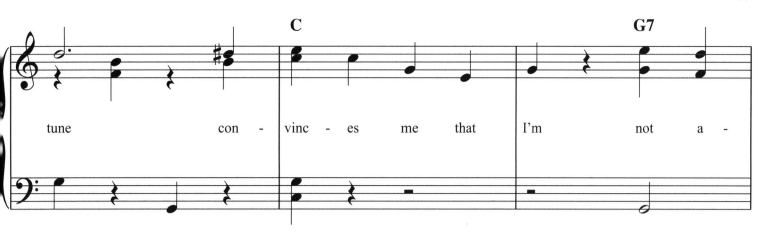

C · · · · · G7

tune con - vinc - es me that I'm not a -

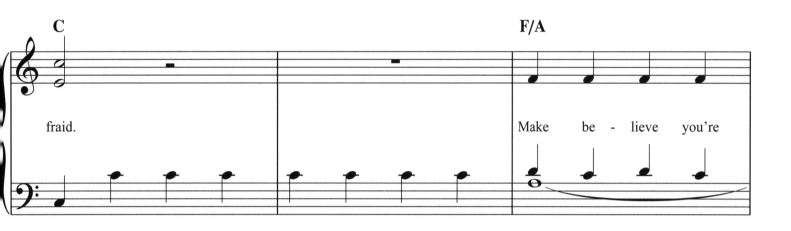

C · · · · · · · · F/A

fraid. Make be - lieve you're

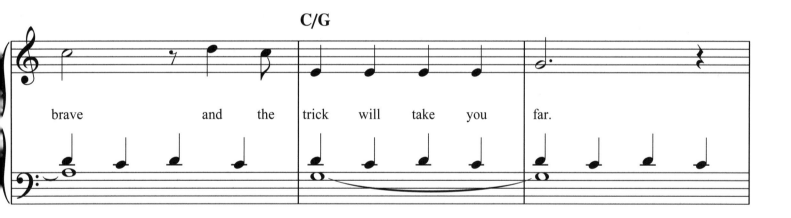

· · · · · · · · C/G

brave and the trick will take you far.

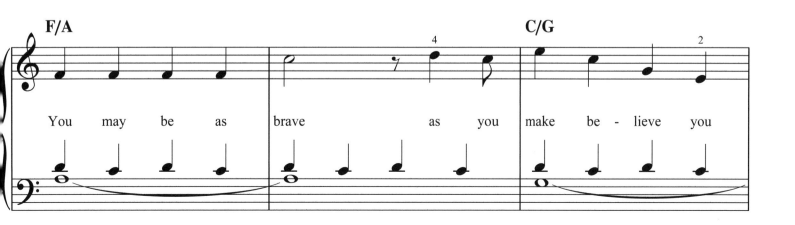

F/A · · · · · · C/G

You may be as brave as you make be - lieve you

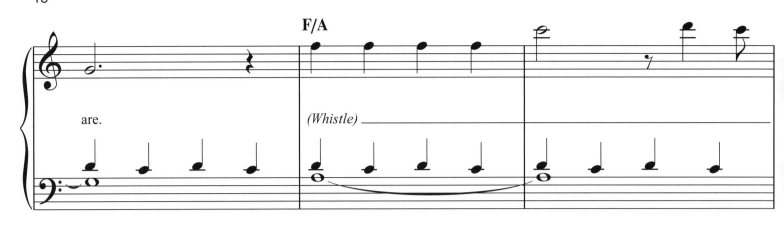

are.

F/A

(Whistle)

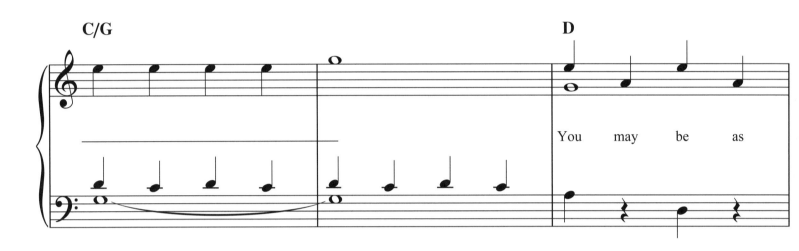

C/G

D

You   may   be   as

Dm

G7

brave   as   you   make   be - lieve   you

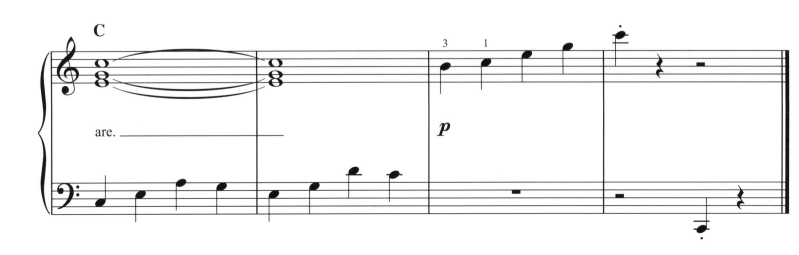

C

are.

p

3   1

THE MARCH OF THE SIAMESE CHILDREN

Music by RICHARD RODGERS

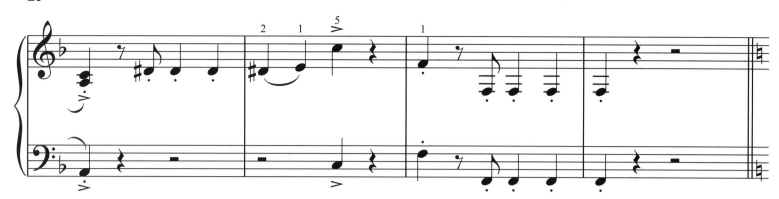

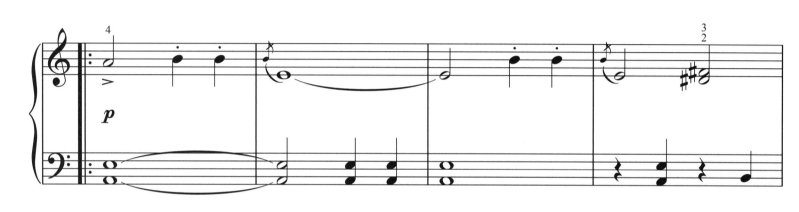

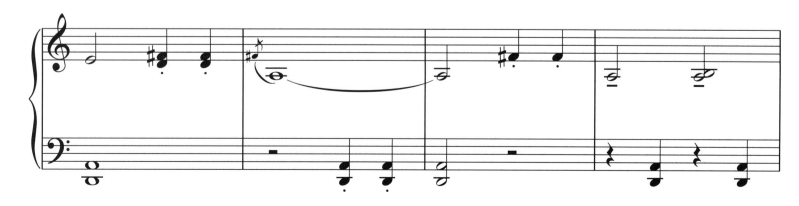

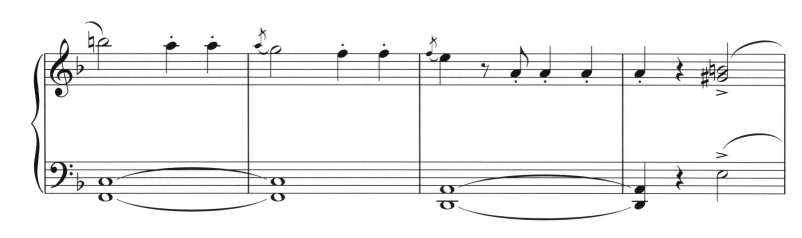

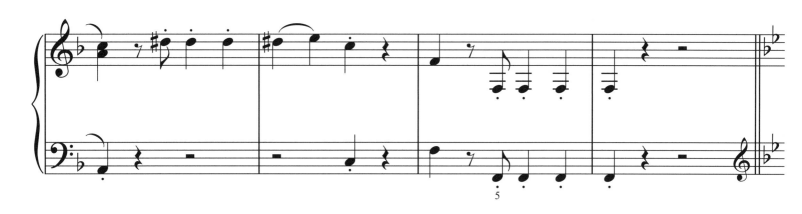

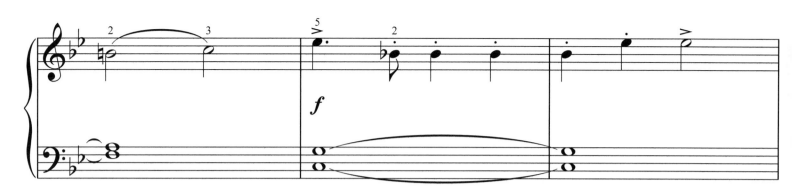

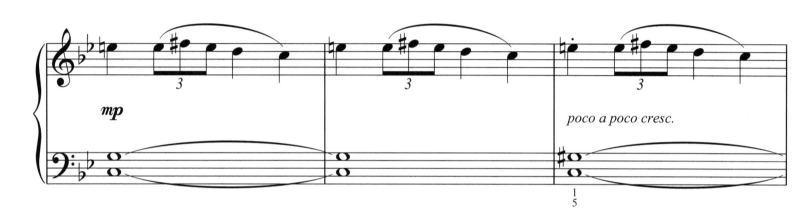

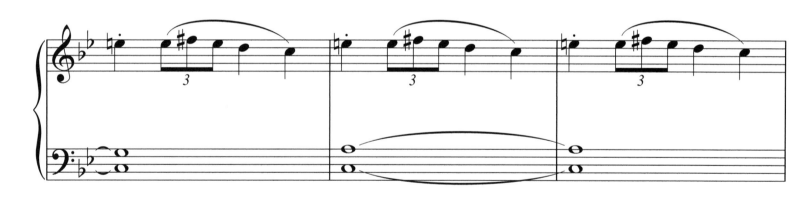

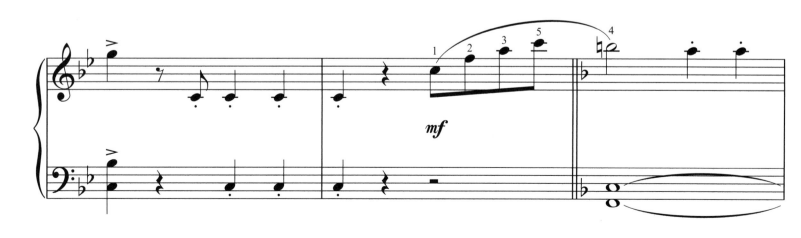

MY LORD AND MASTER

Lyrics by OSCAR HAMMERSTEIN II
Music by RICHARD RODGERS

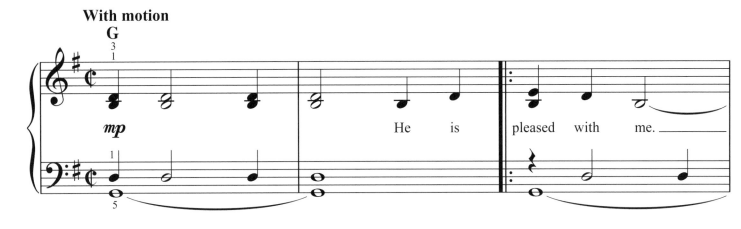

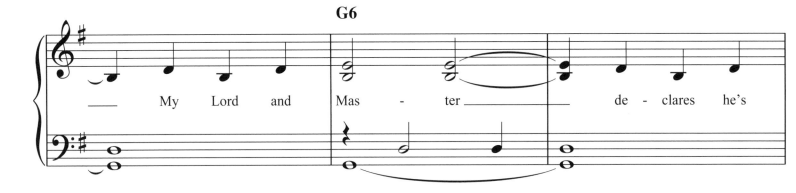

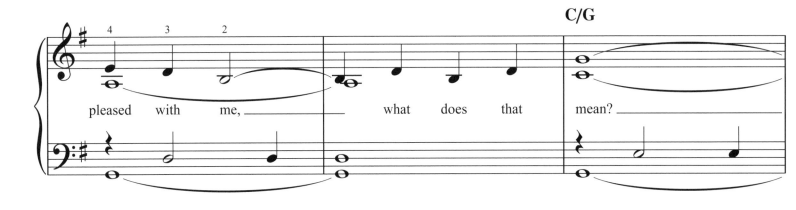

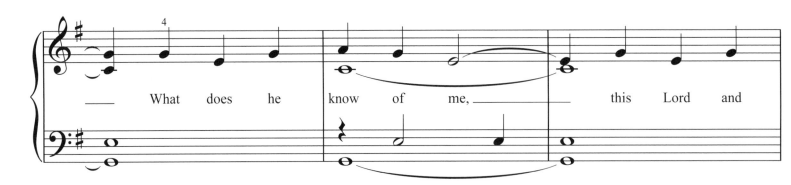

Mas - ter? _____ When he has looked at me, _____

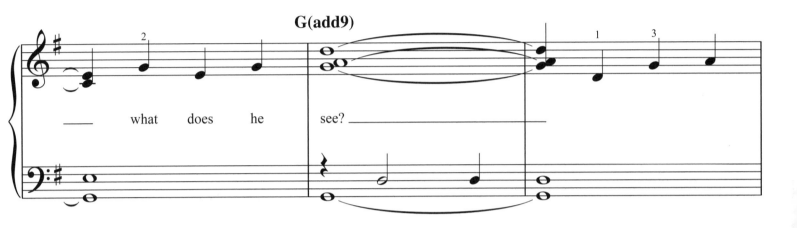

_____ what does he see? _____

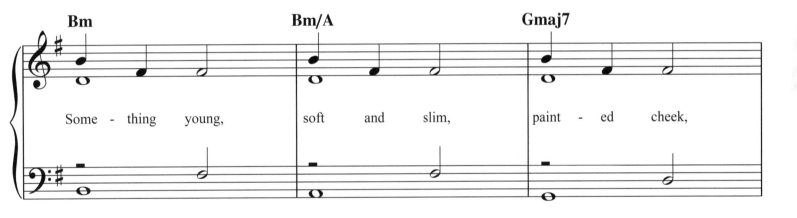

Some - thing young, soft and slim, paint - ed cheek,

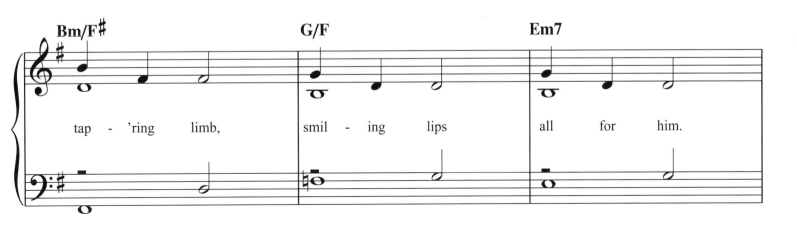

tap - 'ring limb, smil - ing lips all for him.

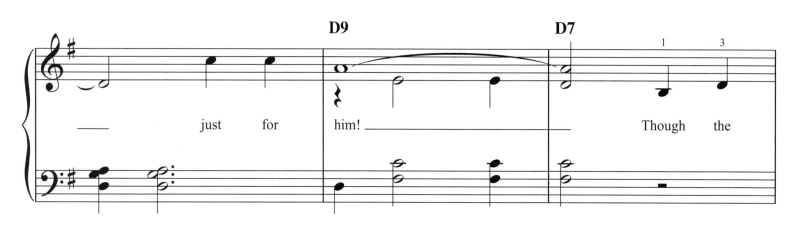

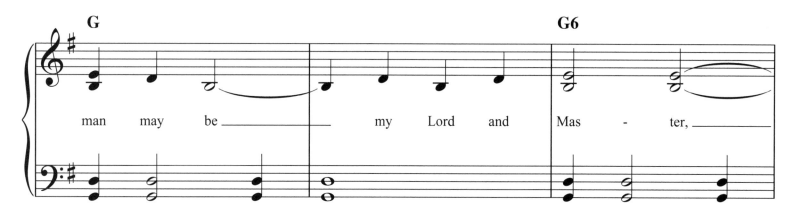

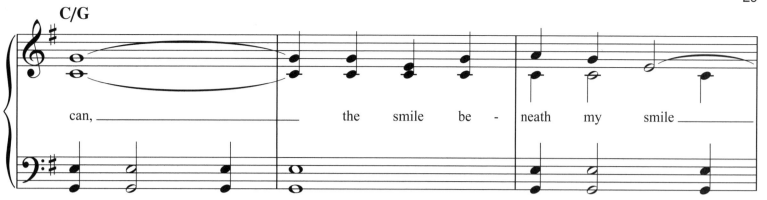

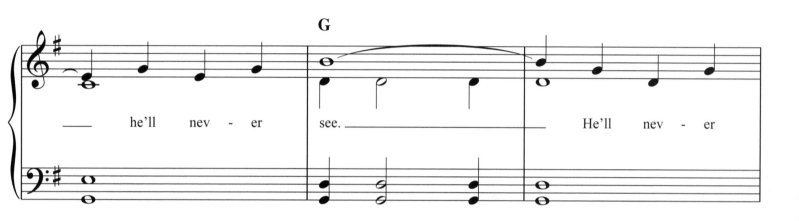

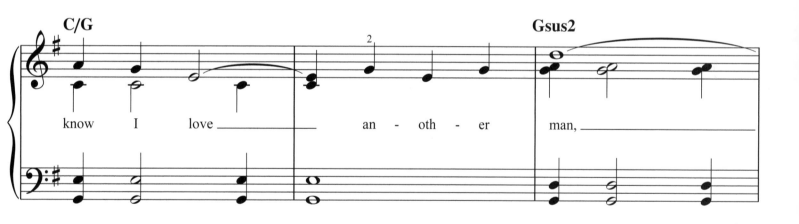

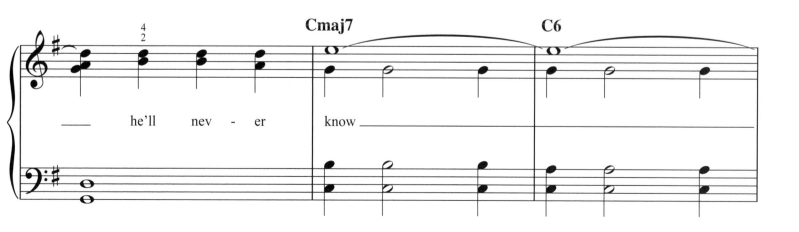

A PUZZLEMENT

Lyrics by OSCAR HAMMERSTEIN II
Music by RICHARD RODGERS

Meno mosso
N.C.

Some things near - ly so, oth - ers near - ly not. There are

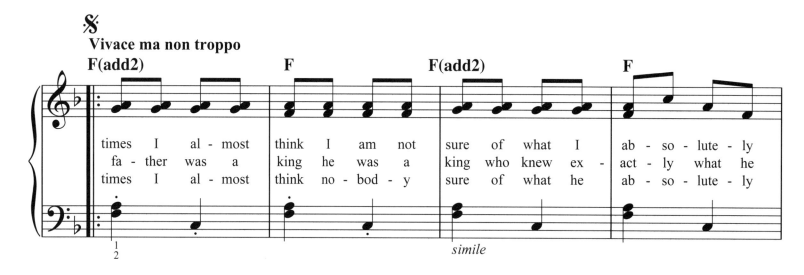

Vivace ma non troppo
F(add2)   F   F(add2)   F

times I al - most think I am not sure of what I ab - so - lute - ly
fa - ther was a king he was a king who knew ex - act - ly what he
times I al - most think no - bod - y sure of what he ab - so - lute - ly

simile

C7

know. _____ Ver - y
knew, _____ and his
know, _____ ev - 'ry -

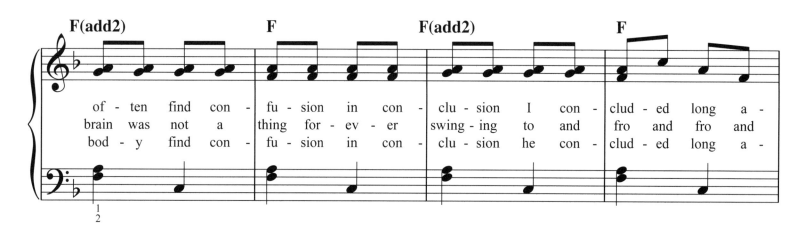

F(add2)   F   F(add2)   F

of - ten find con - fu - sion in con - clu - sion I con - clud - ed long a -
brain was not a thing for - ev - er swing - ing to and fro and fro and
bod - y find con - fu - sion in con - clu - sion he con - clud - ed long a -

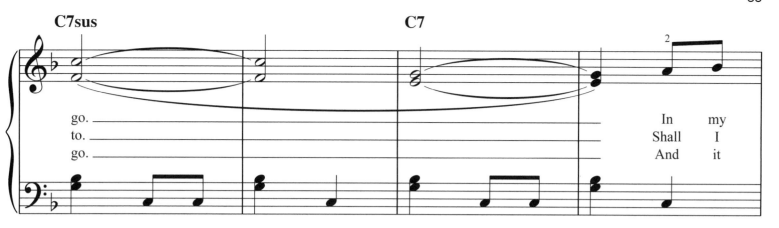

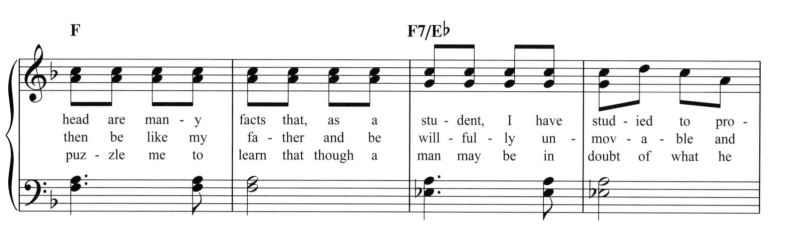

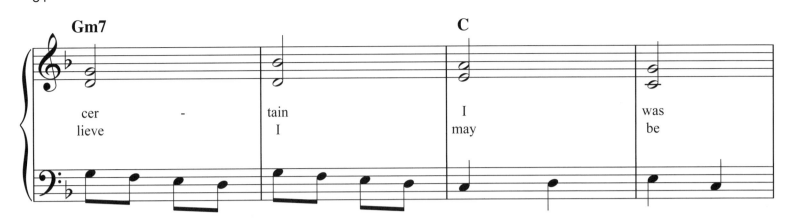

cer - tain I may was
lieve I may be

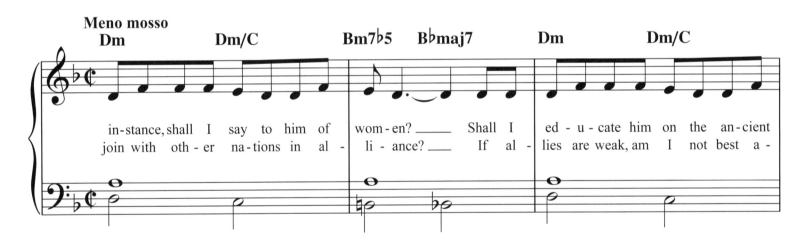

sure. What, for
wrong? Shall I

Meno mosso

in-stance, shall I say to him of wom - en? _____ Shall I ed - u - cate him on the an - cient
join with oth - er na - tions in al - li - ance? _____ If al - lies are weak, am I not best a -

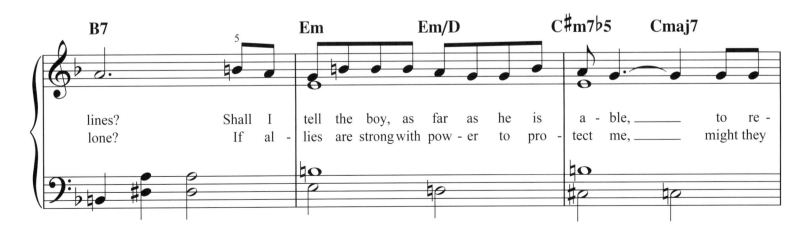

lines? Shall I tell the boy, as far as he is a - ble, _____ to re -
lone? If al - lies are strong with pow - er to pro - tect me, _____ might they

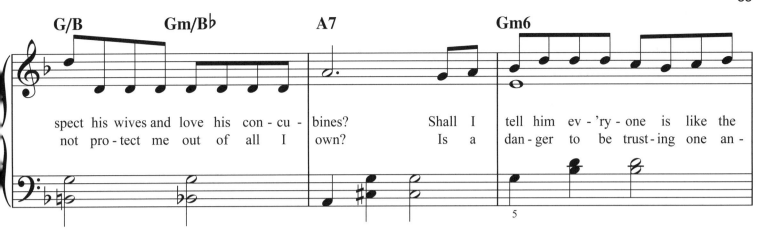

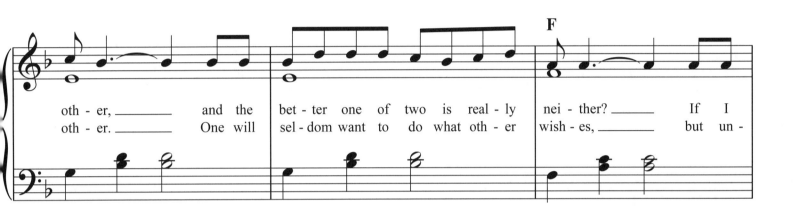

CODA

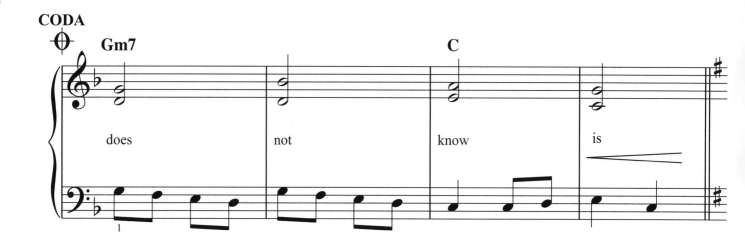

Gm7   **C**

does   not   know   is

G6

so.
f

Gsus2

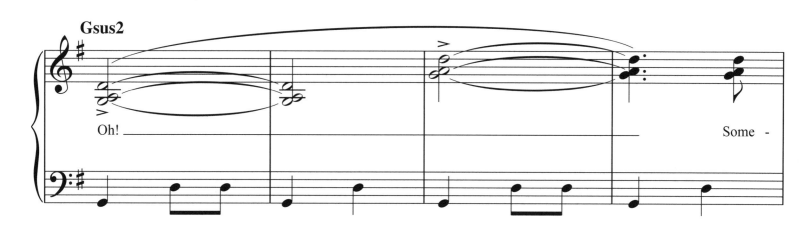

Oh! _____ Some -

D7sus   **Gsus2**

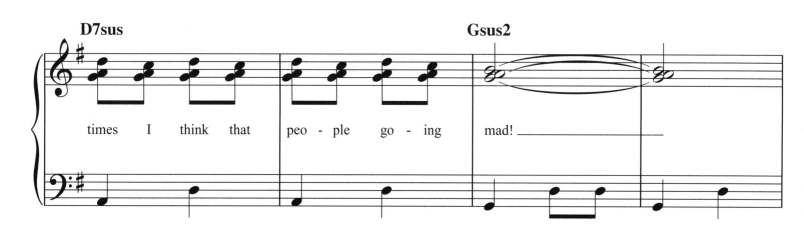

times   I   think   that   peo - ple   go - ing   mad! _____

Ah! _____ Some -

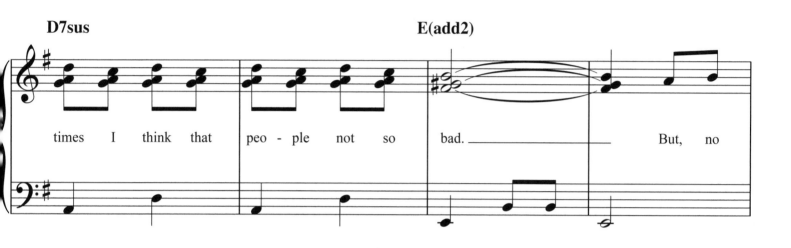

D7sus   E(add2)

times I think that peo - ple not so bad. _____ But, no

Am   Bm   Am/C   Bm   Am   Bm   Am/C   Bm

mat - ter what I think, I must go on liv - ing life. As a

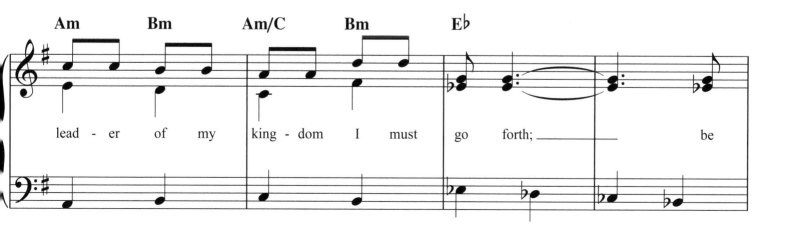

Am   Bm   Am/C   Bm   E♭

lead - er of my king - dom I must go forth; _____ be

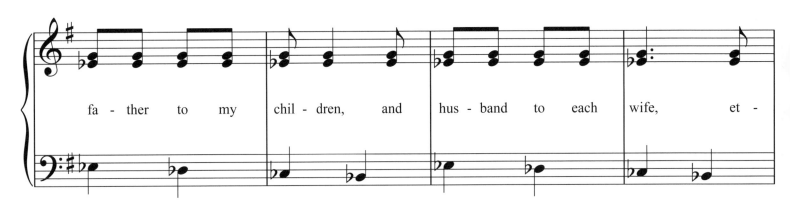

father to my children, and husband to each wife, et -

G

cet - er - a, et - cet - er - a, and so forth. _____

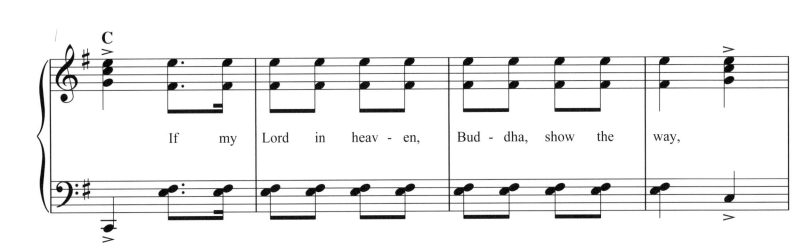

C

If my Lord in heav - en, Bud - dha, show the way,

F#7

ev - 'ry day I try to live an - oth - er day.

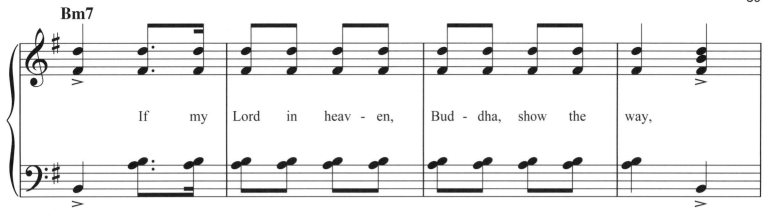

If my Lord in heav - en, Bud - dha, show the way,

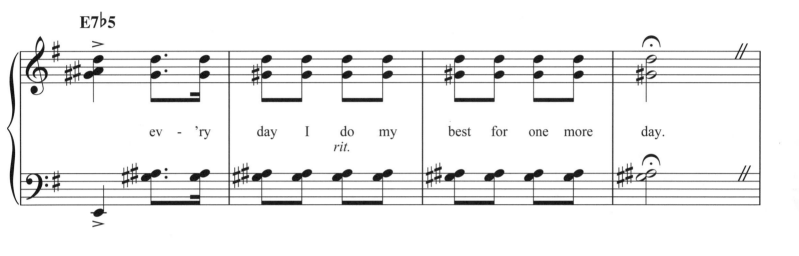

ev - 'ry day I do my *rit.* best for one more day.

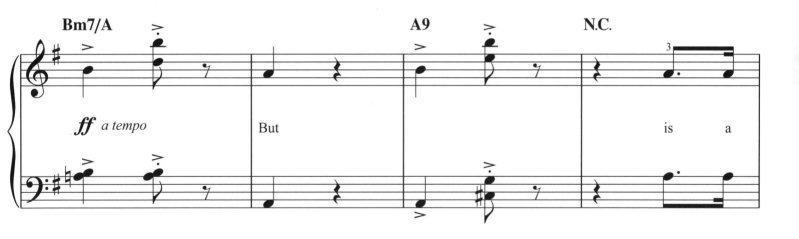

ff *a tempo* But is a

puz - zle - ment! ___

SHALL I TELL YOU WHAT I THINK OF YOU?

Lyrics by OSCAR HAMMERSTEIN II
Music by RICHARD RODGERS

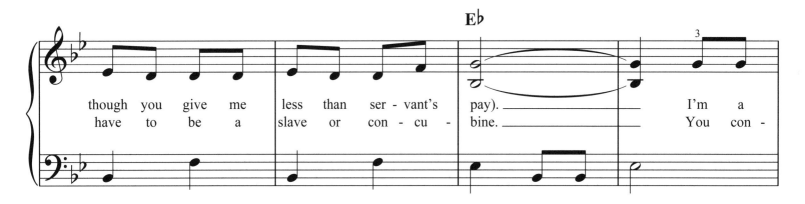

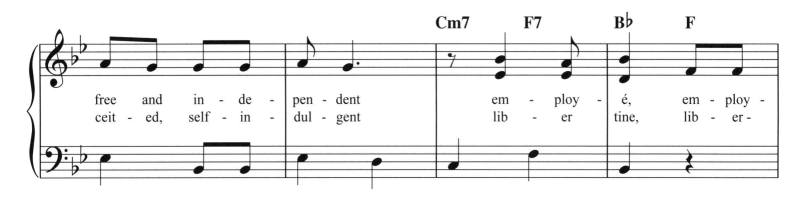

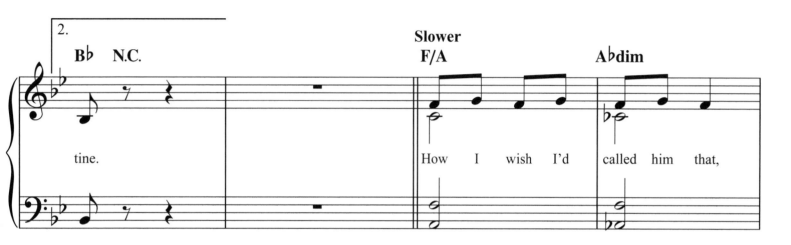

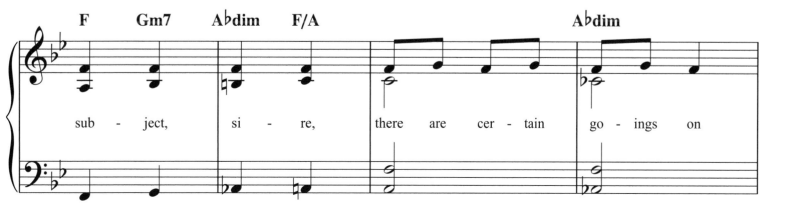

a - round this place, that I wish to tell you I do

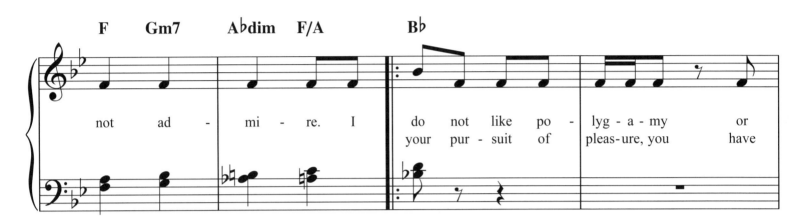

not ad - mi - re. I | do not like po - lyg - a - my or
|| your pur-suit of pleas-ure, you or have

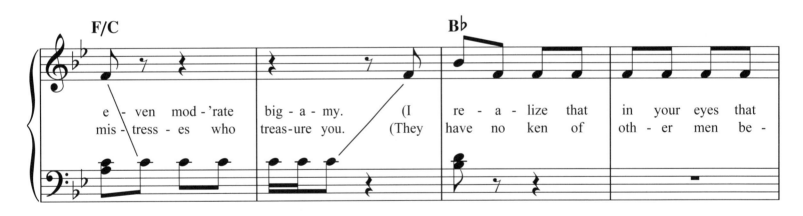

e - ven mod -'rate big - a - my. (I re - a - lize that in your eyes that
mis-tress - es who treas-ure you. (They have no ken of oth - er men be -

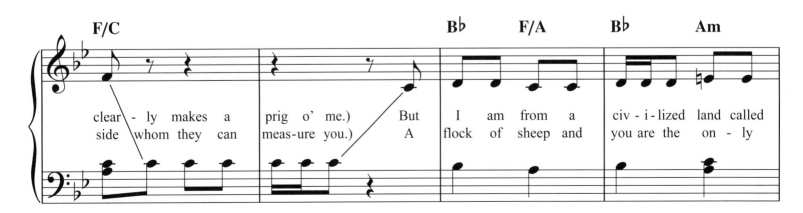

clear - ly makes a prig o' me.) But I am from a civ - i - lized land called
side whom they can meas-ure you.) A flock of sheep and you are the on - ly

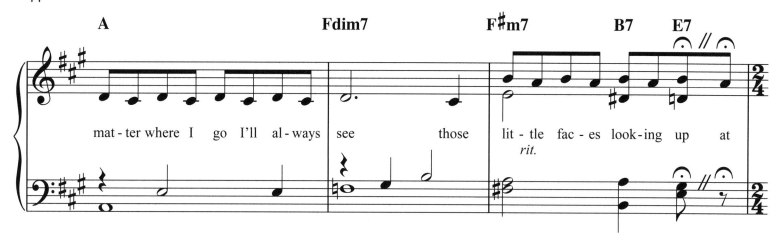

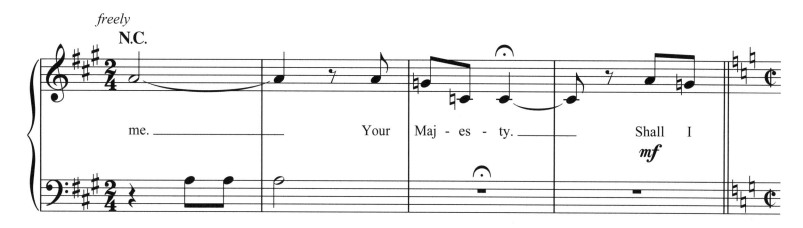

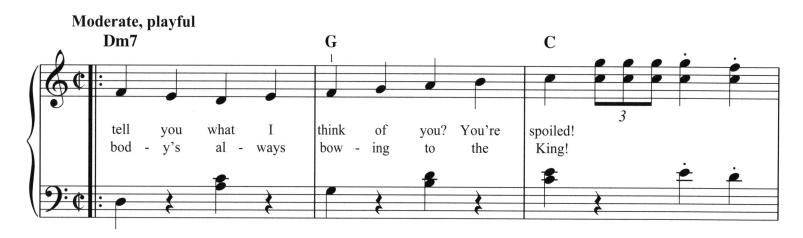

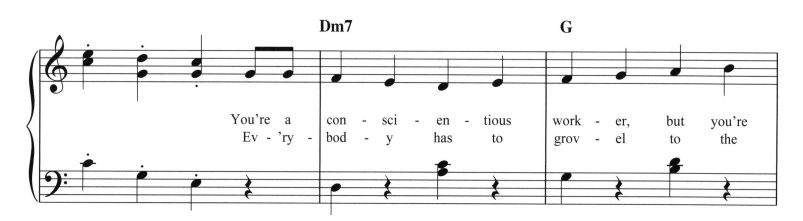

A **Dm7** **G7/D**

spoiled.
King!

Giv - ing cred - it where it's
By your Bud - dha you are

Em7 **Am7/E** **Dm7** **G7/D** **Em7** **Am7/E**

due, there is much I like in you, but it's
blessed, by your la - dies you're ca - ressed, but the

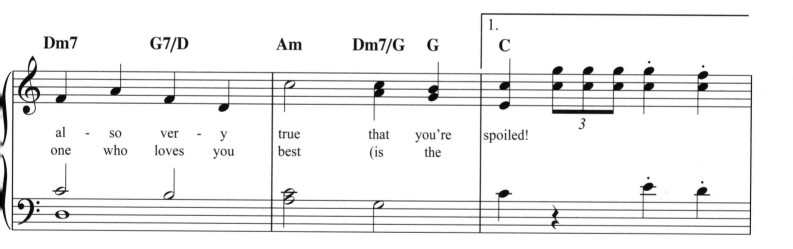

Dm7 **G7/D** **Am** **Dm7/G** **G** **1.** **C**

al - so ver - y true that you're spoiled!
one who loves you best (is the

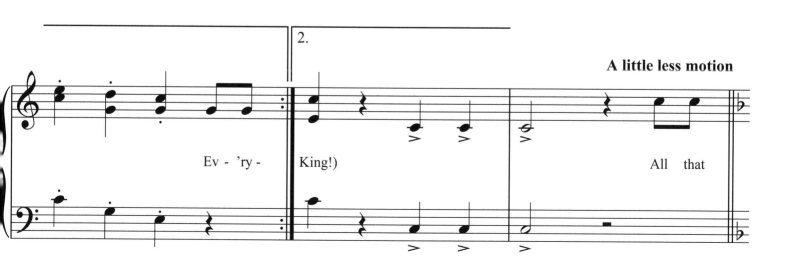

2.

A little less motion

Ev - 'ry -
King!)

All that

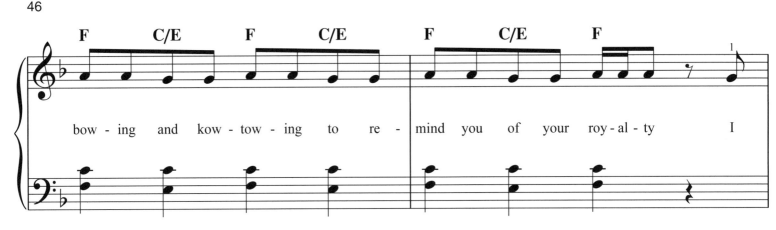

bow - ing and kow - tow - ing to re - mind you of your roy - al - ty I

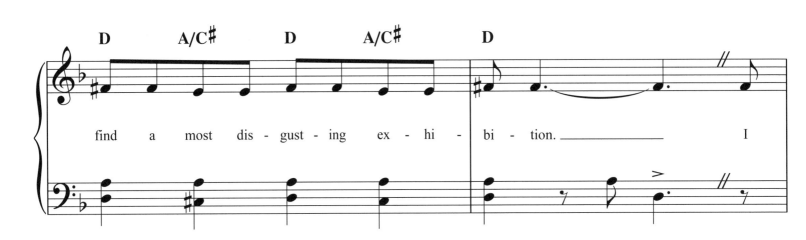

find a most dis - gust - ing ex - hi - bi - tion. _____ I

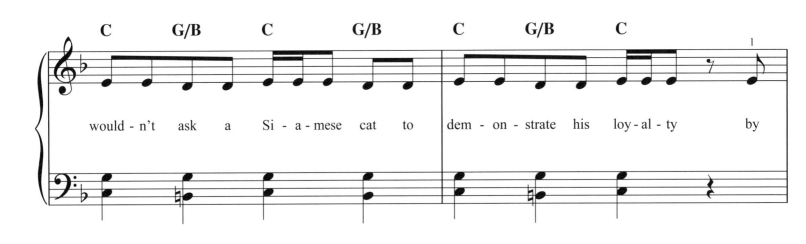

would - n't ask a Si - a - mese cat to dem - on - strate his loy - al - ty by

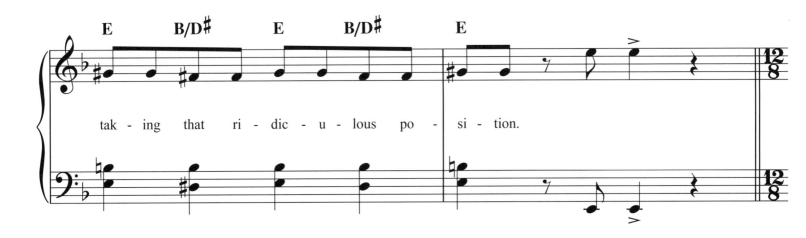

tak - ing that ri - dic - u - lous po - si - tion.

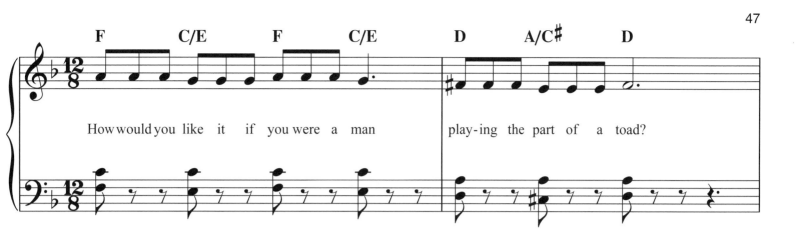

How would you like it if you were a man playing the part of a toad?

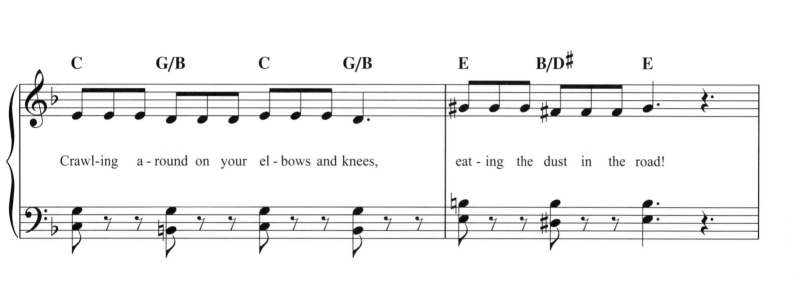

Crawl-ing a-round on your el-bows and knees, eat-ing the dust in the road!

Toads! Toads! All of your peo-ple are toads!

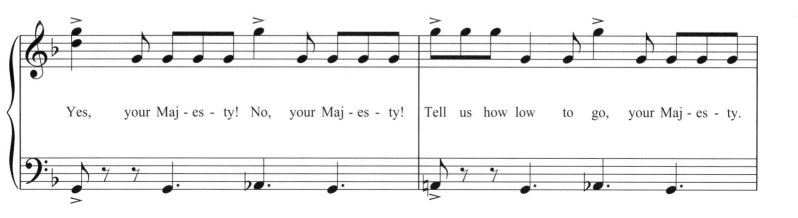

Yes, your Maj-es-ty! No, your Maj-es-ty! Tell us how low to go, your Maj-es-ty.

make some more de-crees, your Maj - es - ty. Don't let us off of our knees, your Maj - es - ty.

Give us a kick if you please, your Maj - es - ty. Give us a kick if you would, your Maj - es - ty.

poco rit.   *molto rit.*

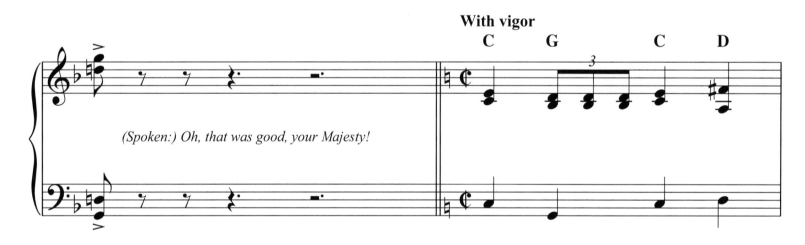

With vigor

(Spoken:) Oh, that was good, your Majesty!

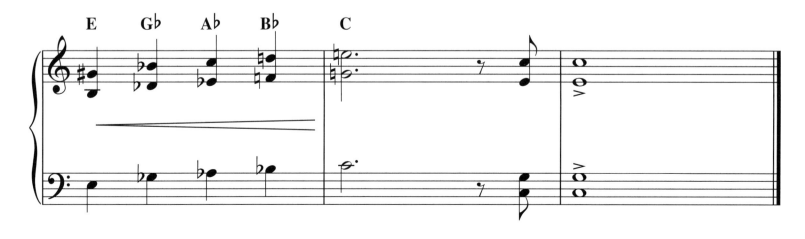

WE KISS IN A SHADOW

Lyrics by OSCAR HAMMERSTEIN II
Music by RICHARD RODGERS

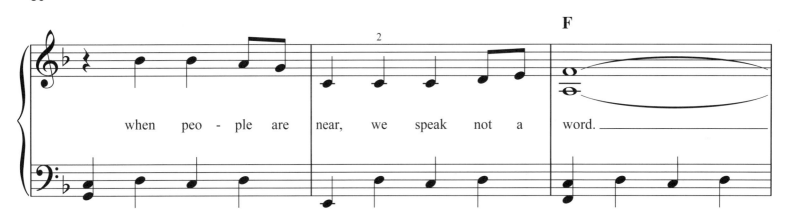

when peo - ple are near, we speak not a word. _____

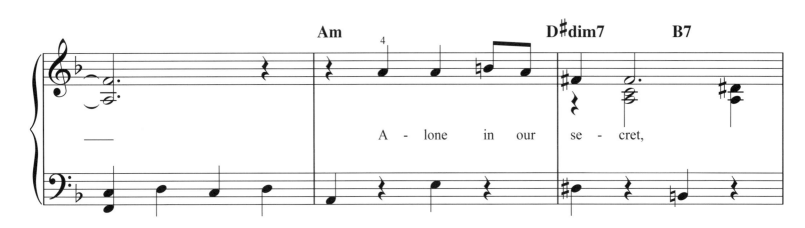

_____ A - lone in our se - cret,

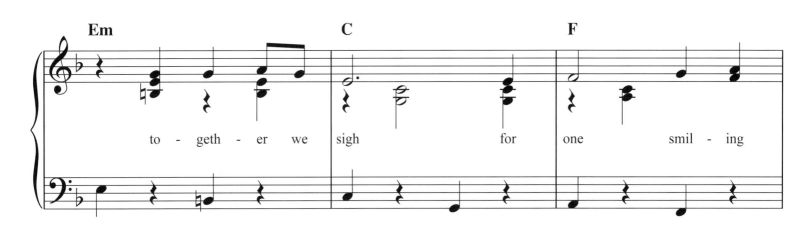

to - geth - er we sigh for one smil - ing

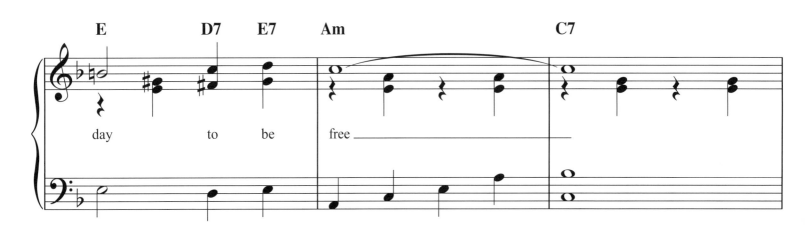

day to be free _____

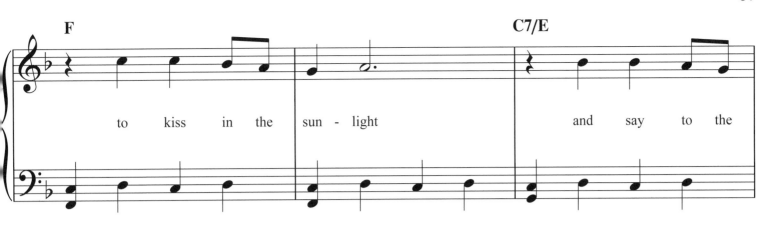

F   **C7/E**

to kiss in the sun - light   and say to the

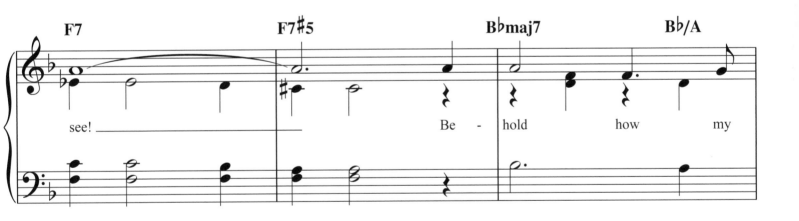

sky: _____   be - hold and be - lieve what you

F7   **F7#5**   **B♭maj7**   **B♭/A**

see! _____   Be - hold how my

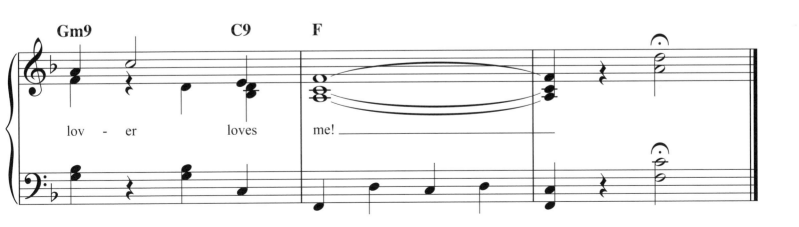

Gm9   **C9**   **F**

lov - er loves me! _____

SHALL WE DANCE?

Lyrics by OSCAR HAMMERSTEIN II
Music by RICHARD RODGERS

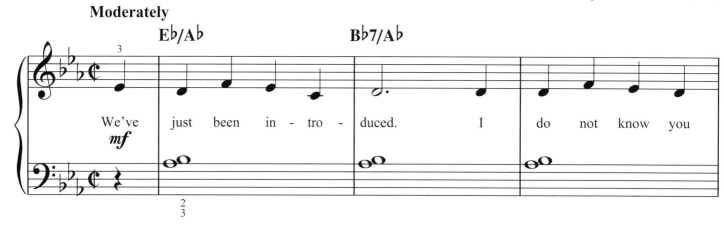

We've just been in-tro-duced. I do not know you

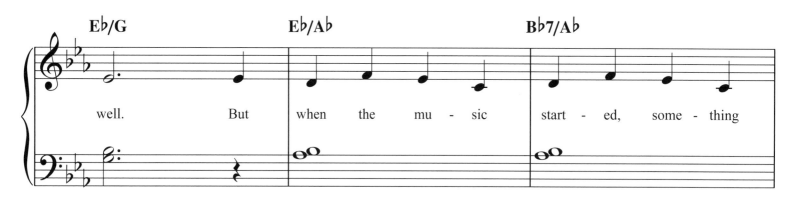

well. But when the mu-sic start-ed, some-thing

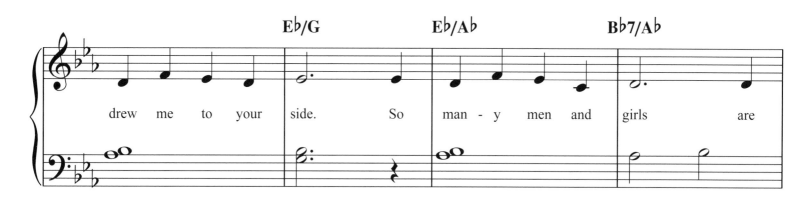

drew me to your side. So man-y men and girls are

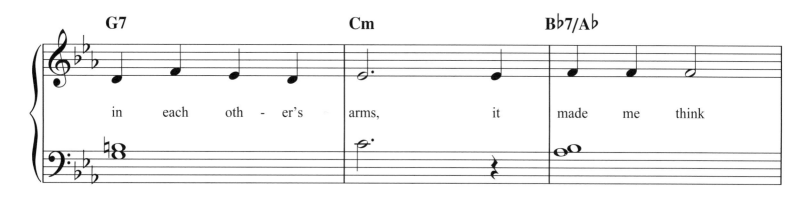

in each oth-er's arms, it made me think

we might be sim - i - lar - ly oc - cu - pied. Shall we

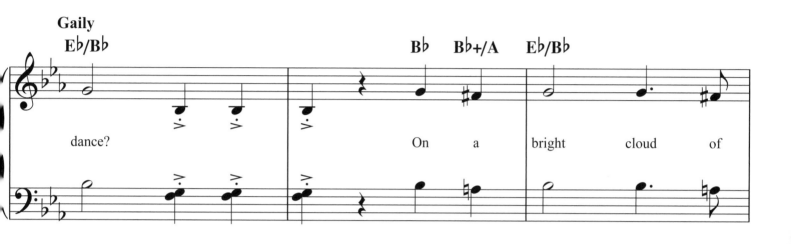

Gaily

dance? On a bright cloud of

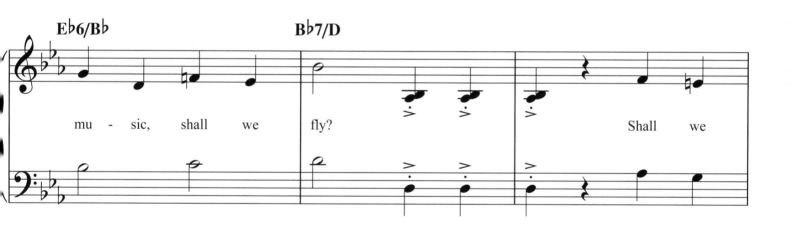

mu - sic, shall we fly? Shall we

dance? Shall we then say, "Good -

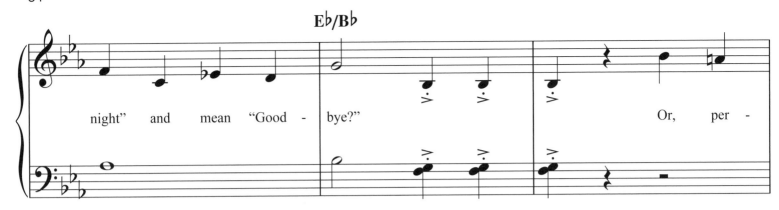

night" and mean "Good - bye?"   Or, per -

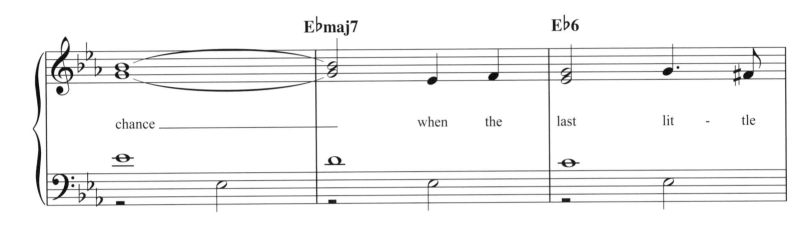

chance _____   when the   last   lit - tle

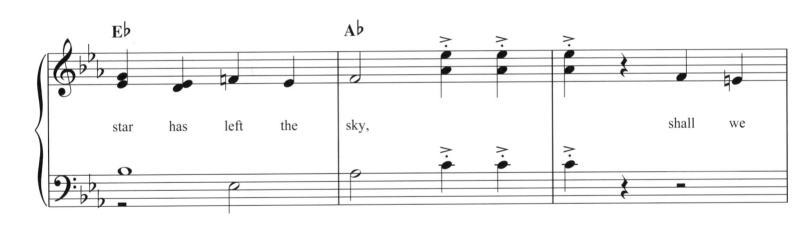

star   has   left   the   sky,   shall   we

still   be   to - geth - er   with   our   arms   a - round   each

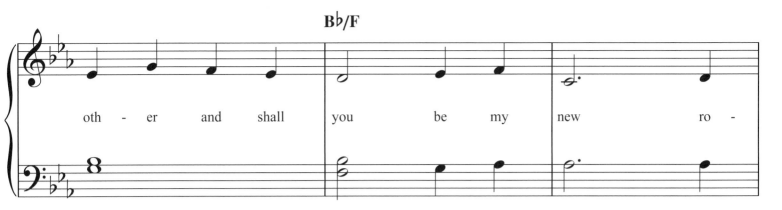

oth - er and shall you be my new ro -

mance? On the clear un - der -

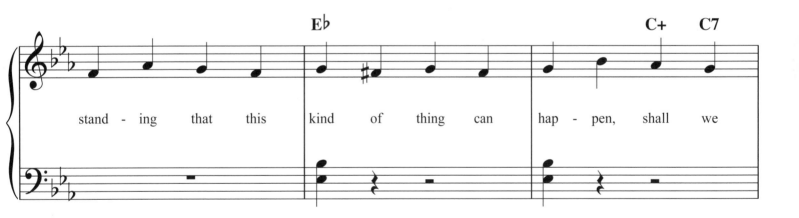

stand - ing that this kind of thing can hap - pen, shall we

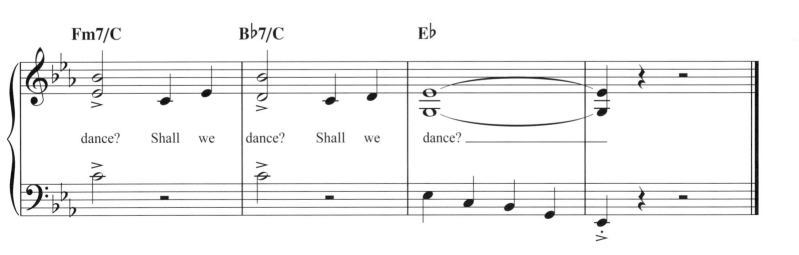

dance? Shall we dance? Shall we dance?

SOMETHING WONDERFUL

Lyrics by OSCAR HAMMERSTEIN II
Music by RICHARD RODGERS

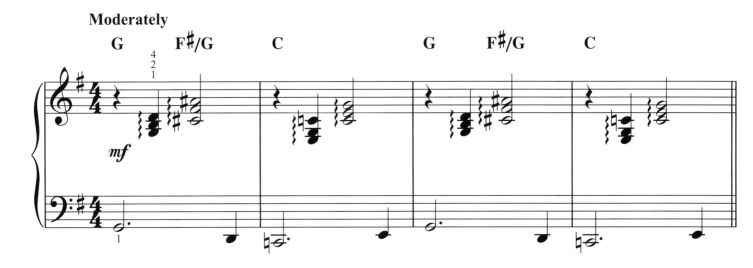

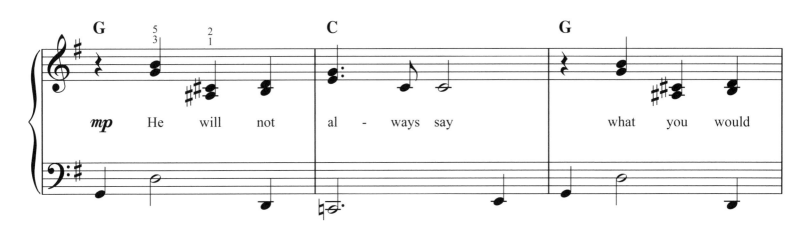

He will not al - ways say what you would

have him say, but, now and then, he'll say

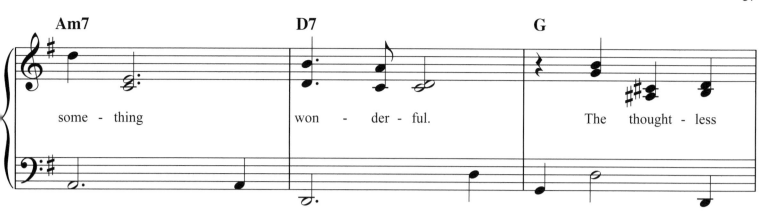

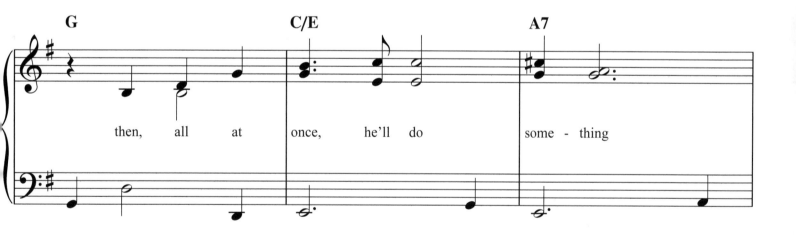

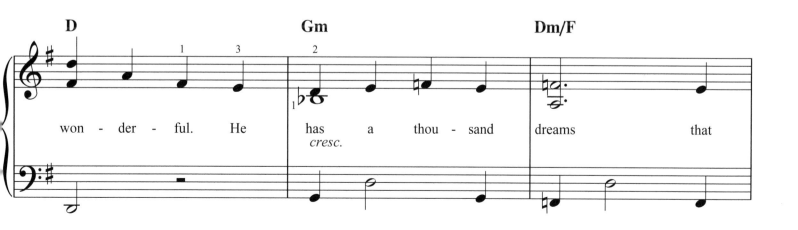

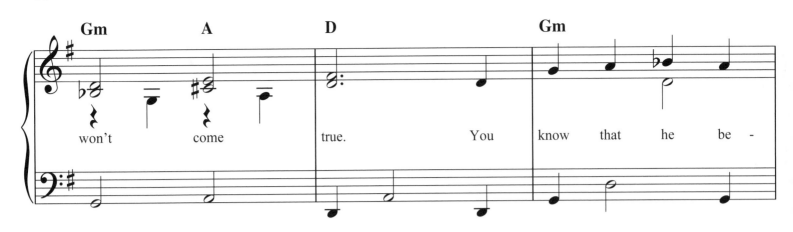

Gm   A   D   Gm

won't   come   true.   You   know   that   he   be -

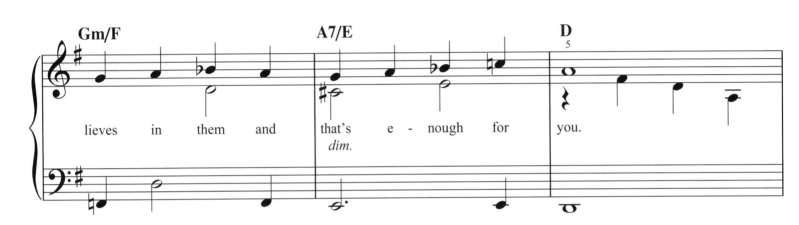

Gm/F   A7/E   D

lieves   in   them   and   that's   e - nough   for   you.

dim.

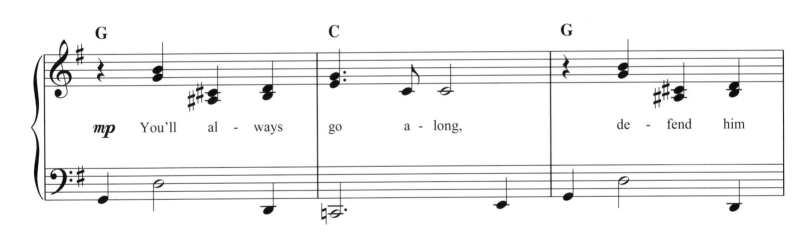

G   C   G

mp   You'll   al - ways   go   a - long,   de - fend   him

C   G   C/E

when   he's   wrong   and   tell   him   when   he's   strong,

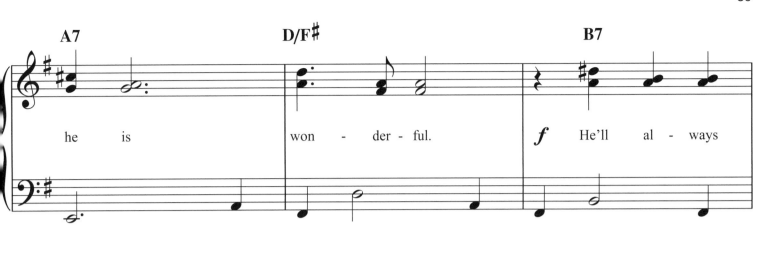

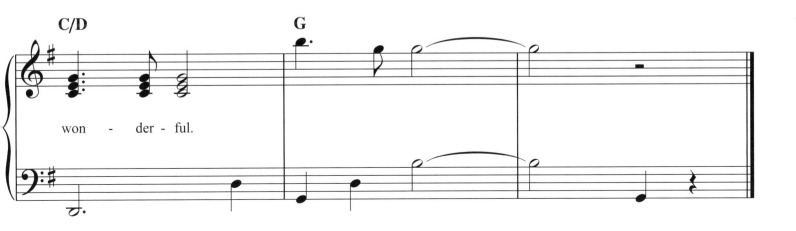

WESTERN PEOPLE FUNNY

Lyrics by OSCAR HAMMERSTEIN II
Music by RICHARD RODGERS

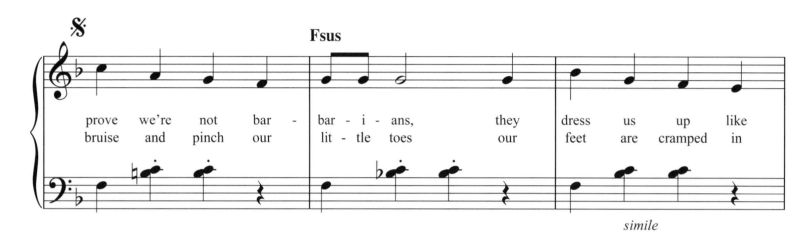

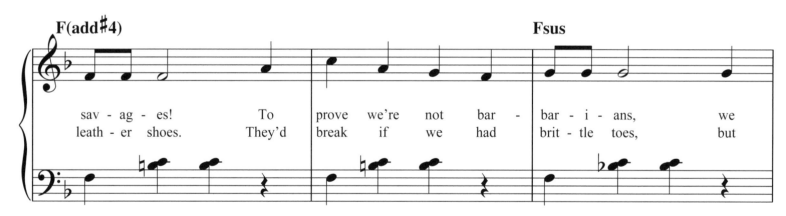

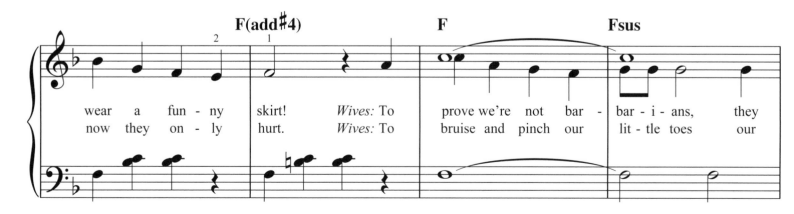

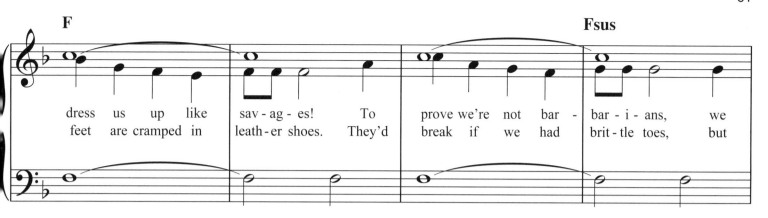

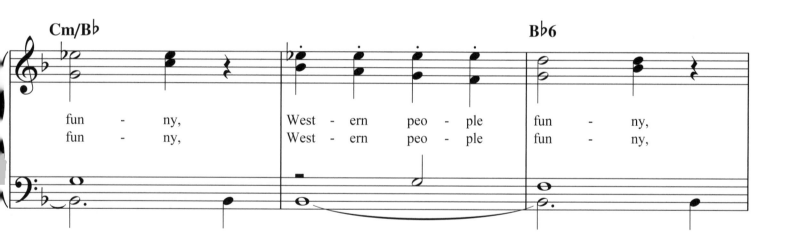

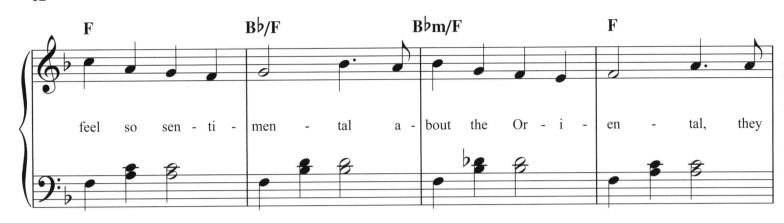

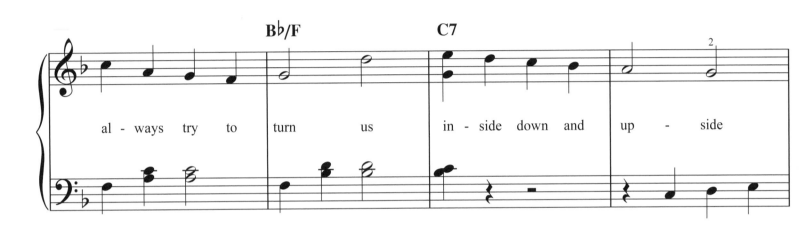

CODA

Bb/F ... Eb/Bb ... Ebdim/Bb ... Bb

true! *Lady Thiang:* They think they civ - il - ize us when-

Eb/Bb ... Ebdim/Bb ... Bb ... Eb

ev - er they ad - vise us to learn to make the

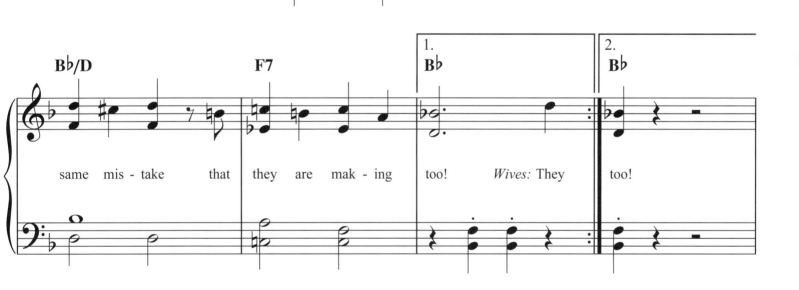

Bb/D ... F7 ... 1. Bb ... 2. Bb

same mis - take that they are mak - ing too! *Wives:* They too!

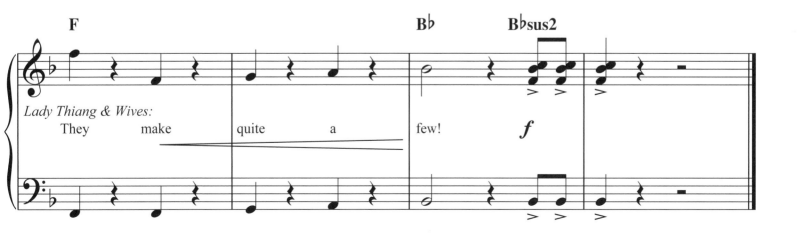

F ... Bb ... Bbsus2

Lady Thiang & Wives:
They make quite a few! *f*